Elizabeth Started All the TROUBLE

Remembering Ellen Levine and Karen Auster Levy —D. R.

For my dear Kris —M. F.

First Edition, February 2016   10 9 8 7 6 5 4 3 2 1

H106-9333-5-15305   Printed in Malaysia

Library of Congress Cataloging-in-Publication Data

Rappaport, Doreen. Elizabeth started all the trouble / by Doreen Rappaport; illustrated by Matt Faulkner.—First edition.

pages   cm

ISBN 978-0-7868-5142-3—ISBN 0-7868-5142-2

1. Women's rights—United States—Juvenile literature.   2. Suffragists—United States—Juvenile literature.   3. Women social reformers—United States—Juvenile literature. 4. Stanton, Elizabeth Cady, 1815–1902—Juvenile literature. I. Faulkner, Matt, ill. II. Title.

HQ1236.5.U6R37 2016

323.3'40973—dc23   2014031824

Reinforced binding

Visit www.DisneyBooks.com

Elizabeth Started All the TROUBLE

By Doreen Rappaport

illustrated by Matt Faulkner

HELP US TO WIN THE VOTE

Disney • HYPERION

Los Angeles   New York

Over 235 years ago, Abigail Adams got a letter from her husband. John was in Philadelphia in a big room with lots of other men. The colonists had declared independence from Great Britain and were busy writing new laws for the new nation.

Abigail was ecstatic. She wanted independence as much as John did. But she was worried: Would women be included in the new laws? She warned John that if women were *not* remembered, they would start their own revolution.

John laughed at her.

It took much longer than Abigail wanted for that revolution to begin. But it finally started, seventy-two years later.

Remember the ladies!

In 1840 Elizabeth Cady Stanton and Lucretia Mott and their husbands traveled three thousand miles across the ocean to London. They were meeting people from all over the world who were working as hard as they were to end slavery.

When they got to the meeting, Elizabeth and Lucretia found out that they were not allowed to be delegates. In fact, if women wanted to be there just to listen to the men speak, they had to sit behind a curtain so they wouldn't be seen.

Elizabeth and Lucretia were shocked. How could men who were against slavery deny women their rights just because they were women? They had to do something to change this.

Well, it took much longer than they would have liked, but on July 13, 1848, Lucretia and Elizabeth met with three friends to plan a meeting in Seneca Falls, New York, to discuss women's rights. The women knew they needed to write some kind of declaration so people would understand what they wanted.

But what should they write?

Elizabeth read aloud from Thomas Jefferson's Declaration of Independence. "We hold these truths to be self-evident, that all men are created equal. . . ."

The women agreed that it was a great document—as far as it went. But Jefferson had left out some very important things. Elizabeth said she would rewrite it. She did, and she gave it a new name: the Declaration of Sentiments.

The women planned a two-day convention to begin six days later. They put a notice about the meeting in a local newspaper. At that time of year in upstate New York, most women were very busy on the farms. The planners didn't think many would come. They were wrong about that.

JEFFERSON

hold these to be self-evident that all men are created equal that they are

Three hundred women came from far and near. By horse. By wagon. Some even walked. The convention had been planned just for women, but when forty men showed up on the first day, the women let them in.

The women didn't feel confident enough to lead the meeting. (In those days, it wasn't considered "proper" for women to lead meetings if men were present.) They asked Lucretia's husband, James, to do it.

For two days, things went along smoothly as one person after another made speeches. Elizabeth read and reread her declaration, paragraph by paragraph, and people discussed what she had written.

Like the male colonists who had listed their grievances against the king of Great Britain, Elizabeth listed all the unfair laws against women written by men. It was a very long list: It *was* unfair that women couldn't go to college or become doctors or lawyers or ministers. It *was* unfair that women could not keep property they inherited. It *was* unfair that women had to give any money they earned to their husbands.

Everyone agreed. No one could deny it. Everything Elizabeth said was true.

But there was lots of debate over Elizabeth's statement that women deserved the right to vote, and it was their sacred duty to get it.

The idea of women voting was too daring for most people at the convention, including many women. Out of three hundred people, only sixty-eight women and thirty-two men signed their names to Elizabeth's declaration. Elizabeth's husband didn't sign. He had left town when she told him what she was planning to say. When Elizabeth's father heard what she had said, he rushed up to see if his daughter was insane.

That's when the big trouble started. It had taken seventy-two years, but just like Abigail had predicted, Elizabeth's declaration started a revolution.

Ministers (all men, of course) spoke out against her ideas.

"Women belong at home."

Newspaper reporters (all men, of course) wrote what they thought about Elizabeth's declaration.

THE PRESS

"A WOMAN IS NOBODY."

"A WIFE IS EVERY THING!"

Lawmakers (all men, of course) laughed.
"Women certainly do not belong in the voting booth."

Elizabeth wasn't surprised that her ideas shocked so many people. Neither was Lucretia. They knew it was going to be a long, hard fight before women won equality. But Elizabeth had no doubt they would succeed.

With so many newspapers all over the country reporting on the Seneca Falls convention, word spread about Elizabeth's ideas. Lots of women agreed with her. Meetings popped up in towns and cities in the North and Midwest. A thousand women came to the first National Women's Rights Convention in Worcester, Massachusetts, in 1850.

Worcester

Albany

Rochester

New York

Cleveland

Syracuse

Philadelphia

Akron

Salem

Cincinnati

Sojourner Truth, who had escaped from slavery, went to a meeting in Ohio. She caused quite a stir when she reminded white women there that black women were treated even worse than they were.

That man over there says that women need to be helped into carriages, and lifted over ditches, and to have the best place everywhere. Nobody ever helps me into carriages, or over mud puddles, or gives me any best place! And ain't I a woman?

In the spring of 1851, a thirty-one-year-old schoolteacher named Susan B. Anthony visited Elizabeth. The two women became fast friends. They traveled everywhere and made lots of speeches together. But after a while it became too hard for Elizabeth to travel. She had to stay home and bake and cook and wash and sew and care for her children and her husband.

Susan B., who was single, went anywhere and everywhere.

Other women hit the lecture trail, too.

Sarah Grimke

Antoinette Brown

Frances Gage

Paulina Davis

Abby Kelley Foster

Ernestine Rose

Angelina Grimke

Susan B. Anthony

Frances Harper

Lucy Stone

THE SUFFRAGE EXPRESS

Soon women started doing what men and even some women called "unladylike" things.

Amelia Bloomer promoted new, comfortable clothing for women. Women could hardly breathe or move before in their tight-laced long dresses with heavy petticoats underneath. Some petticoats weighed as much as fourteen pounds.

And as if Amelia's clothing wasn't "unladylike" enough . . .

Mary Lyon opened a "Female Seminary," known today as Mount Holyoke College. The women studied science and mathematics, geography, rhetoric, philosophy, astronomy, ancient and modern history—subjects that men studied in *their* colleges.

Two sisters, Elizabeth and Emily Blackwell, became doctors. When no hospital would hire them, they set up their own clinic for women and children, and a medical school for women.

Antoinette Brown became a minister and preached in church.

NEW YORK INFIRMARY FOR WOMEN AND CHILDREN

AMBULANCE

AMBULANCE

And then there was Lucy Stone. At her marriage ceremony to Henry Blackwell, one of Elizabeth and Emily's brothers, she refused to say she would "obey" her husband. Henry agreed.

And Lucy kept her name after they were married.

We believe that marriage should be an equal partnership.

In snow. In rain. In hail. The suffragists traveled everywhere. (*Suffragist* is a name for a woman who fought for the vote.) They gave speeches even during blizzards. More times than not, they were mocked and booed by men . . . and by women, too.

But their hard work and dedication helped. In Massachusetts and New York, married women finally gained the right to own property and keep whatever money they earned.

WE WANT THE VOTE.

But no matter how many people the suffragists talked to, and no matter how many petitions they got signed, and no matter how hard they worked to win the right to vote, the lawmakers still refused to change the law.

YES!

YES!

"IF WOMEN VOTE DISASTER AND RUIN WILL OVERTAKE THE NATION!"

WOMEN CERTAINLY DO NOT BELONG IN THE VOTING BOOTH!

"ALL MALE VOTING WAS DESIGNED BY OUR FORE-FATHERS."

CONGRESS

By April 1861, the issue of slavery split the country and led to a civil war between the North and South. Women on both sides of the conflict worked for the war effort, doing more "unladylike" things.

They prepared and delivered supplies to the soldiers.

They lived in tents on the battlefields and fed and nursed the wounded. Some women became spies. A few even dressed as men and fought in battle.

51ˢᵗ Reg

Rose Greenhow
CONFEDERATE SPY

Sarah Edmonds
UNION SOLDIER

Susie King
UNION NURSE

Phoebe Pember
CONFEDERATE NURSE

Pauline Cushman
UNION SPY

Loreta Velazquez
CONFEDERATE SOLDIER

Belle Boyd
CONFEDERATE SPY

Clara Barton
UNION NURSE

Sarah Wakeman
UNION SOLDIER

Sally Tompkins
CONFEDERATE NURSE

On January 1, 1863, President Abraham Lincoln issued the Emancipation Proclamation. It freed over three million black men, women, and children in slavery. But it did not free enslaved African Americans everywhere in the United States. When the North won the war, the suffragists set out to change that. They held meetings and started a letter-writing campaign. They collected more than 400,000 signatures in support of abolition.

On January 31, 1865, the U.S. Congress passed the Thirteenth Amendment ending slavery everywhere in the United States. Then the lawmakers began debating giving the vote to black men.

Now, Elizabeth thought, now is *our* chance to get the vote, too.

But they didn't.

So the suffragists kept on traveling and making speeches. Susan B. racked up the most speeches—more than seventy-five each year for forty-five years. Even people who opposed women voting agreed that Lucy Stone, too, was an especially great speaker.

But the lawmakers didn't listen.

Sojourner tried to vote in Battle Creek, Michigan, and was turned away. Susan B. was arrested and fined when she went to the polls in Rochester, New York. She refused to pay.

Then, hooray for Wyoming! In 1869, women won the right to vote there. Next, in Kansas, then Colorado, Utah, and Idaho! And then in Washington, California, Arizona, and Oregon!

Elizabeth Cady Stanton and Susan B. and Lucy Stone and Lucretia and Sojourner grew old and died. New women continued the fight.

Alice Paul and Lucy Burns were fed up. Sixty-nine years had passed since Elizabeth read her declaration, and women could vote in only nine states.

No more speeches, Lucy said. No more trying to win over male lawmakers. It was time to do something different to get attention. So the suffragists held a parade. On March 3, 1913, a day before President Wilson's inauguration, eight thousand women marched down the streets of Washington, D. C. Following them were twenty-six floats, ten bands, four mounted brigades, three heralds, and six chariots.

Angry spectators shouted ugly names and shoved them. Soldiers had to be called in to stop the attacks. Even people who didn't believe that women should be allowed to vote were outraged at the treatment of the marchers.

The suffragists kept on marching and talking to the lawmakers. More lawmakers listened. Hooray for Montana and Nevada (1914)! Hooray for New York (1917)! Hooray for Michigan, South Dakota, Oklahoma (1918)!

On January 10, 1917, the suffragists started picketing in front of the White House. In rain. In snow. In blistering heat, they stood silently with their signs.

Angry mobs attacked them. The police did nothing to protect them, nor did they arrest any of their attackers. In the next eleven months, more than two hundred women were arrested for picketing. Almost one hundred women served time in prison. Alice Paul was sentenced to seven months and thrown into solitary confinement for two weeks with nothing to eat but bread and water. Lucy Burns and forty other women were beaten.

Other suffragists took their places in front of the White House.

Newspapers wrote about the brutal treatment of the women. Support for their cause grew. A judge finally ruled that the arrests were unconstitutional and ordered the women freed.

A year after the women started picketing, President Wilson declared his support for an amendment to the Constitution giving women the right to vote.

On August 26, 1920, the Nineteenth Amendment, granting women the right to vote, became law. The lawmakers had finally done what Abigail Adams wanted the Founding Fathers to do in that big room in Philadelphia so long ago.

The women had triumphed after battling for the vote for seventy-two years. But they knew their work was not over. There were still many unfair laws to change so that women could have true equality with men.

And we're still working on it.

THE TRAILBLAZERS

Abigail Adams (1744–1818) not only pressed her husband for equality for women, she also insisted that girls deserved an education in public schools.

Elizabeth Cady Stanton (1815–1902), Lucretia Mott (1793–1880), Martha C. Wright (1806–1875), Mary Ann McClintock (1800–1884), and **Jane Hunt (1812–1889)** organized the first women's rights convention in Seneca Falls, New York, on July 19 and 20, 1848. Stanton's "Declaration of Sentiments" became the rallying call for the suffrage movement.

Susan B. Anthony (1820–1906) and **Elizabeth Cady Stanton** formed the National Woman Suffrage Association (NWSA) in 1869.

Antoinette Brown (1825–1921) was the first ordained woman minister in the United States.

Amelia Bloomer (1818–1894) is best known for advocating clothing known as "bloomers," but she was also the publisher of *The Lily*, an important suffragist newspaper, and the president of the Iowa Woman Suffrage Association from 1871 to 1873.

Angelina Grimké (1805–1879) and her sister **Sarah (1792–1873)** left the South because their antislavery views made it impossible for them to live there. They lectured at antislavery meetings and at women's rights meetings.

Sojourner Truth (1797–1883) escaped with her daughter to freedom in 1827 and went to court to get her son back. She threw off her slave name, Isabella Baumfree, and renamed herself. A remarkable preacher, she worked for women's rights and the rights of African Americans.

Lucy Stone (1818–1893) used fiery language and sharp organizational skills for the causes of suffrage and black emancipation, and rewrote the traditional marriage vows to ensure equality between her and her husband, Henry Blackwell.

Elizabeth Blackwell (1821–1910), the first woman doctor in the United States, and her sister, **Emily (1826–1910),** opened a medical practice for women in New York City, and founded the Women's Medical College.

Mary Lyon (1797–1849) founded the first female seminary, now known as Mount Holyoke College, in 1837.

Alice Paul (1885–1977) and **Lucy Burns (1879–1966)** co-founded the Congressional Union for Woman Suffrage.

Carrie Chapman Catt (1859–1947), suffragist leader and president of NAWSA, organized her "army of voteless" women to pressure state and federal lawmakers to give women the vote.

IMPORTANT DATES

March 31, 1776 Abigail Adams writes John Adams, to "remember the ladies."

June 12–23, 1840 Women are barred from participating in the World Anti-Slavery Convention in London.

July 13, 1848 Martha C. Wright, Elizabeth Cady Stanton, Lucretia Mott, Mary Ann McClintock, and Jane Hunt plan the first Women's Rights Convention, held in Seneca Falls, New York, on July 19 and 20.

October 23–24, 1850 The first National Women's Rights Convention is held in October in Worcester, Massachusetts. Annual conferences are held through 1860, except for 1857.

May 28–29, 1851 Sojourner Truth's speech in Akron, Ohio, electrifies the audience.

December 6, 1865 The Thirteenth Amendment, ending slavery, becomes law.

1866 Congress passes the Fourteenth Amendment, which grants citizenship to former slaves and defines citizens as "male." Susan B. Anthony and Elizabeth Cady Stanton form the Equal Rights Association.

1868 The Fifteenth Amendment, giving the vote to black men, passes Congress.

1869 In May, the National Woman Suffrage Association (NWSA) is formed, with Elizabeth Cady Stanton as president. Lucy Stone, Henry Blackwell, and Mary Livermore found the American Woman Suffrage Association (AWSA) in November.

November 1872 Susan B. Anthony tries to vote in Rochester, New York.

1878 The Woman Suffrage amendment is introduced in Congress.

1890 The NWSA and the AWSA merge to form the National American Women Suffrage Association (NAWSA). The focus turns to working at the state level.

1900 Carrie Chapman Catt takes over the NAWSA.

March 3, 1913 The Women's Suffrage parade is held in the capital.

1916 Alice Paul and Lucy Burns form the National Women's Party.

January 10, 1917 The National Women's Party posts the "Silent Sentinels" to picket in front of the White House in support of women's suffrage.

May 21, 1919 The U.S. House of Representatives passes the federal woman suffrage amendment, 304 votes for to 89 votes against. On June 4, 1919, the Senate passes the Nineteenth Amendment with just two votes to spare. The amendment, drafted by Susan B. Anthony and first introduced in 1878 with the same wording, is sent to the states for ratification.

August 26, 1920 The Nineteenth Amendment, called the Susan B. Anthony Amendment, becomes law. It states that "the right of the citizens of the United States to vote shall not be denied or abridged by the United States or by any State on account of sex."

SELECTED RESEARCH SOURCES

Blatch, Harriet Stanton. *Challenging Years: The Memoirs of Harriet Stanton Blatch*. New York: Putnam, 1940.

Flexner, Eleanor. *Century of Struggle: The Woman's Rights Movement in the United States*. New York: Atheneum, 1968.

Griffith, Elisabeth. *In Her Own Right: The Life of Elizabeth Cady Stanton*. New York: Oxford University Press, 1984.

Kraditor, Aileen. *The Ideas of the Woman Suffrage Movement, 1890–1920*. New York: Columbia University Press, 1965.

Stanton, Elizabeth Cady, Susan B. Anthony, and Matilda Joslyn Gage. *History of Woman Suffrage. Vols. 1–3*. Rochester: Charles Mann, 1887; by Susan B. Anthony and Ida Husted Harper. *Vol. 4*. Indianapolis: Hollenbeck, 1902; *Vol. 5–6* by Ida Husted Harper. New York: J.J. Little & Ives, 1922.

Stanton, Elizabeth Cady. *Eighty Years And More: Reminiscences 1815–1897*. New York: Schocken Books, 1971. First published in 1898.

Stevens, Doris. *Jailed for Freedom: American Women Win the Vote*. New York: Boni and Liveright, 1920.

WEBSITES

Women's Rights National Historical Park: www.nps.gov/wori

National Women's Hall of Fame: www.greatwomen.org/women-of-the-hall/view-all-women

Susan B. Anthony House: susanbanthonyhouse.org

If you want to learn more about the women involved in the suffragist movement, read:

Colman, Penny. *Elizabeth Cady Stanton and Susan B. Anthony: A Friendship That Changed the World*. New York: Henry Holt and Co., 2011.

McKissack, Patricia C., and Frederick McKissack, *Sojourner Truth: Ain't I a Woman?* New York: Scholastic, 1993.

Pinkney, Andrea Davis. *Sojourner Truth's Step-Stomp Stride*. Illustrated by Brian Pinkney. New York: Disney • Jump at the Sun Books, 2009.

Stone, Tanya Lee. *Elizabeth Leads the Way: Elizabeth Cady Stanton and the Right to Vote*. Illustrated by Rebecca Gibbon. New York: Square Fish, an imprint of Macmillan, 2010.

AUTHOR'S NOTE

It seems hard to believe today, with girls and young women asserting leadership in so many different fields, that there was a time when women had no real legal rights. In 1848, when Elizabeth Cady Stanton proposed that women have the right to vote—along with many other rights—most people considered her ideas preposterous and controversial. Women who agreed with her were mocked and slandered. Years passed without much outward success, but the suffragists continued their campaign. They were not just fighting for their own rights; they were fighting to change history for all people. The decision to "include" all Americans as real citizens is still unfolding in this country. Remember these women when you need courage!

The quotes and signs in this book have been shortened without changing their meaning. The quotes are attributed as follows: page 5 is from a letter written by Abigail Adams to her husband John on March 31, 1776; page 13 was written by Elizabeth Cady Stanton in July 1848; pages 14, 15, 17, 20, 23 come from *Century of Struggle* by Eleanor Flexner; page 25 quotes are from *History of Woman Suffrage, Vol. 1*; signs on pages 32–34 come from *Jailed for Freedom* by Doris Stevens and from *Century of Struggle*.